Bonding with Our Children in Fun and Easy Ways

Bonding with Our Children in Fun and Easy Ways

Good for Parents and Grandparents Alike!

Marilynn Sambrano, MSW

Art for Book Cover: Benjamin McCoy
Author's Portrait: JC Penney Portrait Studio

Author's Granddaughters
Alex's and Eve's Photo: Marilynn Sambrano

Child's Drawing: Eve

Poets
Garry Gay
Lee Gurga
Alex Sambrano
Eve Sambrano

Computer Assistant: Tracey A. Miles, MS, CMC, Owner, Just 2 Much 2 Do, LLC

Archway Publishing books may be ordered through booksellers or by contacting:

Archway Publishing
1663 Liberty Drive
Bloomington, IN 47403
www.archwaypublishing.com
1 (888) 242-5904

ISBN: 978-1-4808-2462-1 (sc)
ISBN: 978-1-4808-2463-8 (hc)
ISBN: 978-1-4808-2464-5 (e)

Library of Congress Control Number: 2015920938

Print information available on the last page.

Archway Publishing rev. date: 3/30/2016

Many thanks, with love, to Alex, Eve, Steve, Trish, Ilse, Mike and Linda — and the many others who shared their experiences with me.

Author's granddaughters, Alex and Eve, when they were age 4 ½ and 3 years old.

Contents

Preface

These days many parents hold jobs, live far away from their own parents, and/or rarely see their youngsters because the children's schedules are so full. But when we do finally get together, what do we do? Say, "Hi," "What's new?" "Love ya," and "Why did you do that?"—and then we pick up after them and let them watch TV.

There are many things we can do to change our monotonous lives with the kids. In this book we describe many ideas to use whenever we want to show our children and grandchildren that we can be loving and fun at the same time. These ideas and projects cost little to nothing to make and do, and they are easy to accomplish.

Make an impact? You betcha.

Bonding with Our Children in Fun and Easy Ways also includes tips to help us build the confidence we need to be terrific role models for kids. And because our time is precious, this book is quick and easy to read.

We need all the time we can get to show our children and grandchildren that we truly love them—and how clever we really can be.

No Postage Necessary

Become a historian for your grandchildren. No, really do. It's not as difficult as it sounds; in fact, it's a rewarding project to take on. Let me explain.

When I was ten, my aged grandmother sat beside me on the swing on her front porch. She talked and talked about her younger days, including how frightening her boat trip was when her family—my family—emigrated from Europe to America. How sad it is that that's all I remember from that afternoon. After all, ten-year-olds are ten-year-olds, so I didn't think to make a note of the conversation. If someone had written about her thoughts and feelings, the details would have been mine for the rest of my life—and for generations to come.

Write letters to your grandchildren. Tell them what chores you had when you were young, how much allowance you got, when you started dating, when you got into trouble at home or in school, and what your lifetime dreams were. Tell them about things that happened when you were a teenager. I loved to play tennis (though I wasn't very good at it) and catch 'em in the park (and accidentally gave my older sister, Joan, a bloody nose because I was running so fast). And when I was a young adult, I traveled all over to Egypt, China, England, and France. I have lots of stories to share with my granddaughters. Tell your grandchildren, in detail, some interesting and sometimes funny things that happened to you when you were young.

You'll need a place to store these letters. You could choose a sewing box for your granddaughter or a tackle box for your grandson. Or vice versa. Or a box that you personally decorated for each child. Then slip each letter into the box to be read by him or her many years from now.

The bond between you and your grandchildren will carry on forever—no postage necessary.

Be a Good Sport

One day I was a good sport. I didn't think so at the time, though. The girls were four and six years old when they got a three-story playhouse. They were up there all the time. One windy day they wanted me to come up with them. "Will you play with us? Nana, will you? Nana, come on. Please?"

This time, I have to admit I knew no limits when it came to responding to their requests … just ask my arthritis!

"Please come up," they pleaded. It came from their hearts, so I couldn't resist.

"Sure," I said with a grin. "Where are the steps?"

"There aren't any!" they shouted. "We'll help you up!"

Hmm. Help me up?

The only ways to the second floor were a knotted rope, a rugged stone wall, and a bumpy slide. I chose the rope. To make a long story short, after having checked to make sure no adults were watching, up the rope I went. (That sounds fast and easy, but believe me—it wasn't. And I was glad we only went up to the second floor!) Then we played school, where I learned all about money and banking. My four-year-old granddaughter was my security blanket; I clung to her the entire time.

I hadn't intended to be a good sport that day, and I won't go up there again. But my granddaughters felt that I was the best grandmother ever, and that's all that counts. Be a good sport, Grandpa. Try something challenging!

By the way, I left via the slide. And it sure was fun all the way down!

Build a Finch Nest

Here's a good spring project. You and your children are going to put your hands in some mud, but it will be worth it.

We built a nest for a house finch. This clever little bird lives throughout the lower forty-eight states and uses just about anything it can find to make its nest: plastic straws, soda bottle caps, string, buttons, dry leaves, sticks, ribbon, plastic bags, feathers, and ballpoint-pen caps. The children looked outside and around their rooms to find small odds and ends for this project, and I used small stuff that I'd found at the bottom of my purse.

We first made a ball of mud. Then we used some of the mud to form a bowl-shaped nest that would sit atop a base that is made from the rest of the mud. Then the girls pressed all their findings inside and outside the nest. These two never thought a bird nest would look like this!

They firmly placed the nest in a strong fork of branches in a tree (a strong bush would work too) and watched from a distance to see whether a finch would make the nest its home. They knew the birds might not use the nest this year, but the girls could always try again next spring.

Lift a Rock

When the weather is warm, take the kids outside and lift a large rock. You'll be surprised at what you'll find under it: little spiders, tiny ants, large ants, and quick-moving whatchamacallits. A little research in an insect book will tell you something about these hidden creatures, and the kids will learn that a good, dry place to call home can be found under a rock.

If your grandchildren jump when a critter runs in their direction, remind them that humans look like scary giants to those little guys. Now don't you jump—or at least try not to. If you do, you'll have some explaining to do.

On a Lovely Day

———————◆———————

Take the kids outside on a lovely day. My grandchildren and I lie on the grass, side by side, and watch the clouds. I show them how clouds at different levels often move at different speeds and directions from one another. I also tell them that clouds are made of water and that the dark ones hold rainwater that might come down and get us wet. In fact, some rain never hits the ground. And sometimes the sun shines on clouds and makes beautiful colors.

Some clouds form shapes. Clouds aren't stationary—they change shapes, disappear, or appear from nowhere. Little Eve found a dog up there, while Alex discovered an X that soon became a flower.

Peace and quiet. Mmm … and a little education too.

Like Us, Robins Have to Find Food Too

On an early evening in spring or summer, quietly sit on the porch or in the yard with your grandchildren. Soon enough, some robins will come out for dinner. They will alight and then stand very still. Before you know it, they will either move ahead in jumps or walk the way we do—one foot in front of the other. Soon after, they will stand still again.

Then they will turn their heads sideways and look down at the ground. They will search for their dinners, and they will "watch" with their feet as well as with their eyes, for they feel the tiny tremors caused by insects and worms that are moving either underground or on the surface of the grass and weeds.

Robins aren't the only birds that do this, so wherever you live, you'll be able to find other birds that search for food as robins do.

Although preschoolers' attention spans are shorter than ours, even they are able to look where we point and understand when we tell them that the robins are looking for their dinners.

Sharing nature with kids is rewarding for all of us.

Take Me to the Car Wash

One day Alex went out with her girlfriends for a bike ride. Little Eve wasn't invited to play with the older girls, and she sat weeping at the door. She had nothing fun to do. Was there anything I could do to help her out?

I wondered aloud, "Could there be anyone who might want to clean my car?" Eve sat up perfectly straight, and her tears immediately stopped. She could do it and have a ball while her sister was just riding her bike!

I banged around with the bucket—a bit of positive noise adds to the fun. "Do you know where the rags are?" She sure did! Whenever water is involved, so are kids.

I spelled out the rules and made sure she followed them. Her scratchy shoes had to be lined up by the garage door. She couldn't move any dials or the gearshift. I then made sure that she knew where all the very dirty areas were located. I really wanted her to have fun. She was especially excited because my convertible's top was down, and that meant she could walk from the front seat to the back without hitting her head. She said that was really fun!

Little Eve grinned the whole time she worked. Her jealousy of her sister disappeared with a swipe of a wet rag. She missed spots, but I didn't say a word. I didn't care. I constantly praised her.

A tip for a job well done? That was up to me. It was a win-win situation for us both. Her braggadocio was worth the work, so money never entered her mind. I did insist that she take a dollar though. After all, she earned it.

You may not have a job like this one, but you can come up with something to do without mentioning the actions of an older sibling. After all, older grandchildren do have interests that are different from the younger ones'. But I have to admit that this job is a great one for any crying child.

Pinpointing Emotions

One day I heard stomping feet on the floor above me. Pretty soon those feet, belonging to my nine-year-old son, came down the steps. Boy, was he angry. I didn't know why, but he was ready to blow up right then and there. I wasn't quite sure what to do about it. Then, out of the blue, I said to him, "You're angry."

Suddenly he settled down. "You bet I am," he said as he sat on the steps. As soon as I had identified his emotion, he quietly began to tell me what was on his mind, and the anger disappeared.

Instead of letting him have it by telling him to settle down, go to his room, or put him on immediate punishment, something inside me reacted in a far better way: I realized he was acting out rather than saying what he was mad about. My son was angry but didn't quite know how to express himself.

My friends and I have been doing this, and it has worked many times. Young children can't think of the words to express their feelings, because they're just not yet part of their vocabulary. There are times when they act out negatively or are at a loss as to how to otherwise express themselves. Even we adults have times when we're lost for words. So what do we do, both young and old? We act out. But by the time we reach parents' and grandparents' ages, we're a little better at finding words.

Many times, helping our youngsters find the right words can turn into hugs, and that means some bonding is taking place! And that's a win-win situation for all. We have to remember not to scold our children when they finally discover what it is they're trying to say. A word or two might be needed, and that will often do the trick.

The Beauty Shop Contest

It was a hot summer day, and both of us grandmothers were visiting the girls. We were groaning out on their deck, wondering if it might be nicer inside where the air-conditioning was on. But the girls had an idea of their own.

"Let's have a contest," one said with a grin.

"Just sit here and we'll get everything we'll need," the other added.

Off they ran inside, giggling while they put their idea together.

Before we knew it, we grandmothers had bath towels around our necks. And then the fun began. The girls turned our chairs around so we couldn't see each other, and we were told not to look at each other. It was a "Beauty Shop Contest," with the winner being the sister who was the most creative with "her" grandmother's hair.

Now, both of us grandmothers have thin hair that does its own thing.

We laughed because we believed there could be no winner; even professional hairdressers have little luck with us.

Bowls of warm water were placed on the table between us, and our hair was washed and dried just a bit. I felt swirls of hair behind my ears, and smaller swirls going across my neck. Soon Alex started putting large ones on my forehead. Of course we were getting wet, towels or no towels. How can anyone make hair stay in one place if it's dry?

The girls laughed the whole time they "worked." Then they decided the contest was over. Our chairs were turned around so we could see our "opponent." What a hoot! Mirrors were provided, and after we took good looks at ourselves, we checked out the other grandmother. Eve's style gathered the other grandmother's hair into what looked like a ponytail growing out of the top of her head!

We all won that contest because we were all laughing on our way to the freezer, where ice cream was waiting for all of us!

Ah, Such Imaginations

It was an East Coast summer day: the heat and humidity were stifling. Even so, our granddaughters were determined to ride their bikes. I followed them out the door. I had a broken bone in my foot, so there were other places I'd rather be—but you and I know about the unwritten mandate of grandmothers ...

I sat on a bench under a small tree. It was only after I saw sweat coming from beneath the girls' helmets that I realized that I too was soaking wet. My car was nearby, so I shouted, "Come on—let's take a break."

They readily jumped off their bikes and got into the car. My five-year-old granddaughter, Eve, took over the driver's seat, and her seven-year-old sister, Alex, sat in back with me. Although it was hot in the car (the engine wasn't on but the doors were wide open, bringing the hot air in), nobody complained.

Pretty soon Eve decided we were going to take a trip on a plane and that she was the pilot. Alex wasn't paying much attention to her because she had discovered some bags behind the backseat. They contained things I'd planned to give to a charity shop, but before you knew it, Alex was rifling through them.

Eve put on a Mickey Mouse hat that Alex had thrown to her, and the ride began. "All right, y'all, buckle up because we're goin' to Disney World." (I don't know where that accent came from.) We in the backseat laughed as we buckled up for the trip.

Pilot Eve spoke to the tower through an invisible microphone, and then she shouted, "Here we go."

Meanwhile, their mother brought out cold drinks, which were much appreciated by the three of us.

As Eve turned the steering wheel back and forth, she pointed out all the sites below. Meanwhile, Alex continued to dig around in the bags. "Sit down," the pilot ordered.

After that journey ended, the pilot switched to wearing a cowboy hat (again, thanks to her sister), and we were off on a bus ride. "Bring your tickets up front. Ya need a ticket. Y'all need one. Where to?" Eve asked.

"Kentucky," called out Alex.

Eve's response was loud and clear: after she tapped her new hat down, she yelled, "Kintucky, here we come."

After Alex got off the bus (even though she stayed in the car), the driver asked me where I wanted to go. Colorado was my choice.

"All right, here we go. Sit down and don't talk so loud," demanded Eve. She described the countryside as we traveled. Her given "facts" weren't always right, but who cared? What fun we had taking those trips!

We had spent an hour on our plane and bus rides, not even aware of the heat. It was then that the girls noticed my swollen foot, and they quickly became nurses. With their help and kind words, I limped along between them—in their wonderful world of imagination. We went inside the house-hospital, where they tended to me as nurses.

Every chance you get, "ride along" with the kids. My magical rides started with Mickey Mouse piloting an airplane. This was an hour I'll never forget.

Gosh, I'll have to start keeping a journal …

Drawing Feelings

Late one spring afternoon our four-year-old granddaughter, Eve, was having lots of fun swinging. It began to get chilly, so I told her she needed to wear a sweater. Saying no, she swung as high as she could. I pulled the swing to a stop and took her, kicking and yelling, into the house.

I sat her down at the kitchen table and put a pencil and a piece of paper in front of her. Wow, was she angry! Neither of us said a word.

Pressing down as hard as she could, Eve drew a stick figure with a face with teeth on all sides of its square mouth. She scribbled a "word" and then asked me how to spell "Nana," my nickname. She then signed her drawing and pushed the paper over to me.

We broke out in peals of laughter. We laughed and laughed. She ran around to my side of the table and gave me a big hug.

"Read me a book, Nana," she called out as she danced into the living room.

How beautiful can a granddaughter be?

Come Walk with Me

You and I know how crucial it is to be able to trust others. There's a simple thing you can do to help your grandchildren develop this important trait. You're going to take her on a "trust walk." Its explanation is easy: tell her that together you're going on an adventure during which she will be blindfolded. She then has to guess what she's touching during the walk. Be sure to let her know that there will be no tricks ahead and that you'll make sure she'll be safe from tripping or running into something. You needn't tell her you're helping her with trusting others. That might take the fun out of it.

Put her arm in yours and slowly walk around outside. With her free hand, have her touch whatever you place it on. She can examine it (for example a tree trunk or a rock) and try to guess what it is. She can describe it but not remove her blindfold until the walk is over. She'll become more confident as you move on.

After all is done, you two will have a good laugh. You'll know you've helped her trust you and then others (of course after her parents talked to her about not trusting those who might hurt her and learning the warning signs of dangerous people approaching). But she's only thinking about having walked with you, not about trust. It slips to the back of her mind, and when trust is needed, it'll come to the forefront.

Think of how many positive things we put into our kids' minds. Awesome!

Shhh ...

It's coming to the end of a nice day. No matter how cold it is, head out to the porch with the kids—pajamas, terry robes, teddy bears, and all. Then look to the west. Magnificent, isn't it? As the sun drops toward the horizon, its colors become awesome. It takes only a few clouds to magnify the sun's hues of orange and red.

Shhh ...

Absolute bliss is taking over. And the closer it comes to the horizon, the deeper the sun's colors get. Stunning. As calming as a bedtime story. Or a glass of red wine for you.

Lightning Bugs

On a warm summer evening I took our granddaughters out to the backyard. Soon a rhythmic blinking began. There were lightning bugs in the neighborhood. When I first pointed them out to the girls, they jumped up and down with glee.

The four-year-old stopped jumping and got a pensive look on her face. "Look," she slowly said, "they're magic soldiers guarding the forest."

Was this a treat or what!

Ni Hoa *

---◆---

The next time you see your grandchildren, greet them by saying, "Ni Hoa." That's Chinese for hello. One day when I visited Alex at day care, I greeted her and her friends with this phrase, and she and all her classmates thought that was really neat. You can guess which child in the room was as proud as could be. Even now, years later, they shout "Ni hoa" whenever the children see me.

Ask teachers and parents (even you) if they know how to say hello in another language. Even pig Latin would do!

---

* Pronounced "knee how"

Back to School, Nana

What child doesn't want to take charge sometimes? Our granddaughter is no exception, but when she wants to take charge in a big way, and I continue to experience enjoyment even though it's a lot of work for me. Let me explain.

One day eleven-year-old Alex asked her younger sister and me if we would like to play school. "That sounds like fun," I responded, thinking about the subjects I would teach them. But Alex had a different idea: she would be a college professor teaching us about ancient Egypt.

And what a classroom she put together! We had desks (I sat at a small table), and she even made lockers, complete with paper-clip locks, for the handmade doors. She gave us folders and pencils and had her mother make personalized T-shirts by ironing decals with our names and the letters AE on the shirts. That stands for the Academy of Egypt. Alex designed the shirts and had Mom put "Prof" on the bottom corner of her shirt: she is, after all, the professor.

Alex got books from a local bookstore and the library. She even talked her parents into taking a trip to a nearby university that has an extensive display of Egyptian artifacts and mummies. She took notes and drew sketches of what she saw there. And she talked her mother into buying yet another book!

Alex is one professor who is well versed in her subject matter. Soon her nine-year-old sister dropped out of school. The work was too hard for her, and I didn't try to talk her into staying because it was difficult—even for me!

When I see Alex every other week the classes carry on. I've learned so much about this topic—and am given lots of homework! When I asked her if she gets that much homework in school, she said she sure does. While I find that a little hard to believe, I don't argue with her.

We're both having lots of fun, learning much about the topic, and Alex is the adult for a change. This class has lasted at least several months, and who knows how long it will continue or what the next subject will be? I just checked whether Egypt is being covered in her classroom and I'm doing her homework for her. I'm not.

Alex's mom has moved the classroom out of the living room, but Alex hasn't complained. She's acting like an adult.

You can do the same without spending any money. Just be sure your grandchild's heart is in it—and then the teaching begins!

Let's Help Build Their Vocabularies

———◆———

Well, we could think big and start with a make-believe word that's fun to say but has no meaning, like "supercalifragilistic-expialidocious." We grandparents have nothing against make-believe, especially when it comes to our young grandchildren. But think of the fun we can have with words in the world of reality.

Before you start, make yourself a promise: every time you see your grandchildren, you will use one word they've probably never heard before. On long visits you may do this more than once, and his or her parents may do one a day, but let's not raise the bar too high. A little bit of learning goes a long way.

You have a mundane vocabulary? "Mundane" is a good word to use with the kids! "Are we going to have a mundane kind of day to-day?" you might ask. Then see if anyone might venture a guess about the meaning of the word. If there's no response, tell them what it means. Get yourself a thesaurus, so the next time you see the kids, you might say, "I'm elated to see you today." And what a laudable thing that is to have used that word. Now, they may not say anything after having heard a new word or two, but chances are they will ask you what the word denotes.

Sorry, I'm getting carried away. But look at this endeavor this way: you know what college entrance exams are like, so every little word we expose the kids to is bound to help them down the road in one way or another.

We adults don't have to be highly educated to be smart, that's for sure.

What's New in School These Days?

Let's say you want to know how your grandchildren are doing in school. When you ask, they shrug and say, "Okay." But you really want to know how they're doing.

You just asked a yes-or-no question. That's the kind that's quick and simple to answer, one that doesn't require any details if the person you directed the question to doesn't really want to spend time answering it. It's the type of question we parents and grandparents often ask the kids.

On the other hand, open-ended questions are ones such as "Tell me what subjects you like best this year." This question can't be answered with a simple yes or no, which is where you want to be. After your grandchildren tell you what they're studying, you can continue the conversation with more questions, thus opening up the dialogue you want.

Try it, Grandma and Grandpa. They'll learn firsthand that you really care about how they're doing and how important school is to them—and you.

Fill a Folder

B uy a brightly colored folder. As time goes by, between each visit with your grandchildren, be on the lookout for some interesting things to put in it: pictures of animals; words using different fonts found in a magazine or a newspaper; an old photo of the kids' parents; a picture of an unusual bird, such as the spoonbill (a large bird whose bill looks like a spatula). There's a wealth of items that can fit into the folder. Some advertisements, with the help of computers, show clever interpretations of real things: I saw a Dalmatian whose spots were red, and another where many of the dog's spots were on the floor around it!

Take the folder with you when you visit the kids. Fill it with different things each time. Once, I put small pretzels in it. My granddaughters looked forward to filling my—our—folder for nearly a year.

Like most everything else, the children's interest will change, and it's then time to move on to something more challenging for them. And Mom and Dad, you'll have no trouble doing that!

Let's Cook Something Tasty

When I was young, the only things I remember doing in the kitchen were washing and drying the dishes, setting the table, and using cookie cutters for the holidays.

Perhaps my mother was extra cautious with us, or maybe this was the way it was done for all kids my age.

These days we grandmothers often go one step further. We let our kids help put together meals with many different kinds of food. Once, little Eve's Mom had macaroni on the menu, and little Eve couldn't wait to help make one of her favorite dishes. After spreading the unbaked pasta across the bottom of the glass dish, she followed the directions Mom gave her. Eve made the dish all by herself (adding extra of her favorite cheese on top!), and Mom put it in the oven. It tasted mighty good, and Eve was proud of it.

Cookies are another fun thing to bake. With my close supervision, the girls use the mixer. Taking turns is the hardest thing for them, but they manage.

After licking their fingers, the girls rolled out the dough and then pressed the cookie cutters down to make various shapes. They created personalized shapes too, and laid the cookies out on the sheets by themselves.

These days it's easier and quicker and neater to buy cookie dough in premade tubes, but those are not nearly as fun to make as cookies from scratch.

Let's Eat Dinner

Some days our grandchildren can't keep their minds on the food set before them on the dinner table. Try these ideas to help eating become reality.

I SPY: This is a traditional game set for tabletop playing. For each game, someone gets to secretly choose something on the table. The others at the table try to guess what it is. In order to take a guess, some food must be eaten before that person either comes up with a guess or asks for a clue.

Even preschoolers can play. Four-year-old Eve baffled everyone when she picked a tiny fork on a salad dressing bottle. Then the person to Eve's left got the next turn to try to baffle those at the table—but only after having eaten some of her dinner. The game keeps going until dinner is done.

YOU SAY: The first one playing this game takes a bite of food and then says a sentence; the person to her left must start her sentence with the last word of the sentence she's just heard—but only after she's taken a bite of her food.

The game gets silly and sometimes difficult, but everyone has fun with it, and the food is gone just in time for dessert!

The Leftovers Café

While we're talking about food, let me tell you an idea that worked a miracle at our granddaughters' house. A refrigerator full of leftovers can be turned into fun. If you have grandchildren who are elementary school aged, this is just the project for them. Take them aside to make all the plans for their café. They'll love this project!

I did this with seven-year-old Alex and five-year-old Eve, and they had the time of their lives. Alex checked out the refrigerator and made a note of what leftovers were there. Their mom checked to be sure they were edible and not expired. Alex then ran to the computer (boy oh boy, we couldn't have done this when we were young!), and with her mom's help, she printed out a menu.

The girls set the table (little sister Eve thought of putting a glass of water beside each place setting), decided what their restaurant would be called, made a sign for it—The Leftovers Café—and were the waitresses while I worked kitchen detail. I gave them kitchen towels to drape over their arms, and the café was open for business.

Eve seated the patrons, and Alex gave everyone a menu. Alex announced the specials and took the orders. I warmed the food, and the waitresses graciously took it to the diners. Papa had steak, Mom had chicken, and Pat (the other grandmother) had a pork chop. Eve had her beloved spaghetti, Alex had pizza, and I can honestly say I can't remember what I had. Oh, and the girls came up with offering desserts (including ice cream bars and chips) on a tray!

Alex and Eve were happy, I was happy, their mom was really happy, and the rest of the family was delighted. The girls refused token tips—they'd had so much fun that receiving money for their work wasn't necessary.

Lemonade

One day our six-year-old granddaughter, Alex, asked me if I would like her to make me a glass of homemade lemonade. As soon as I said that sounded good to me, she began to seriously work on my drink. She put together water, a squirt of lemonade concentrate, chocolate milk, cinnamon, pepper, raisins, and sugar. She stirred it and stirred it.

"Here, Nana." She smiled proudly. "This is for you."

Just as you would do, I took a sip, said I had never tasted lemonade so delicious, and gave her a big hug. I suggested that she put the remaining drink in the refrigerator so the rest of the family could taste it later. She did so and then went happily on her way, soon forgetting about it. Nothing more was said.

Love in a glass. The best drink I ever had.

Tell a Story

———————◆———————

We all know about storytelling, but do we tell stories to our grandchildren? Turn the lights down low, gather round, and weave a story full of warmth, excitement, and delight. It can be fiction or even a scene from your childhood. You can tell them the whole story or let the kids take turns adding to it. Or each can tell a story or two. What fun they will have in the world of make-believe.

What fun you are, Grandpa!

How about a Joke or Two?

Everybody loves a good joke. Tell a few to your grandchildren to see how much their moods improve. If you don't know any that they would understand, look some up before you see them. There are books in the library that include jokes for young children.

Meanwhile, you could always start with a knock-knock joke. There's the good old owl joke, for example: "Knock, knock." "Who's there?" "An owl." "An owl who?" "Only owls say 'hoo'." Everybody laughs at this one!

Give the children time to make up a joke. They may not be funny, but laugh along with them anyway.

Who says grandparents aren't fun? I'll bet you could come up with one or two very funny jokes.

Set the Stage

————————◆————————

Kids are always acting up, but never fear: this may well be the time to take advantage of their talents. Let them be the stars of a show. They will make up the plot; choose the costumes; make the scenery; decide who will play what; and pick the director. If they have time, they may also want to make tickets for their show. Charging a dime to see an original show doesn't seem like too much to me.

This play doesn't need to have a storyline or a beginning and an end. It can just be an act. Help your grandchildren if they need it. The costumes can be Mom's and Dad's clothes, or include your sweater, or just use what the kids are wearing. The scenery can be as simple as the kitchen chairs. And don't let the director get too bossy. You may plan ahead and bring some items (a purse they've never seen, some jewelry, or old shoes) when you visit. Make sure they come up with a title (try not to help them), and have one of them—not you—be the announcer.

When all is ready, take a seat and enjoy the show! And when it's over, it's probably worth a standing ovation. And while we're at it, let's teach them a new word: "Bravo!"

Our Comments Say a Lot

Something so easy to do can last forever for your children. This is a way for the kids to get to know you better. Short, quiet comments do the trick.

Imagine you're sitting in a room with the kids and they're reading. You can simply say, to no one in particular, "I love to read." Not "I love to read like you do," because when you say it that way, you're only speaking to one child. When you don't aim your comment at just one child, they all take it in. By doing this, the children learn more about you, and also, they learn that what they do is valuable.

The small things you say, Dad, say a lot.

Do They Really Know What We Mean?

It seems as though just a minute ago everything was going very well: The children were playing side-by-side, and there was a buzz of satisfaction in the room. All of a sudden it fell apart. Murmuring grew to loud accusations that grew to sweeping away what another child had been working on … and tears began to flow.

What did I get myself into today? you wonder. As you're giving terse directions about separating the kids and giving out punishments, you're also thinking that there must be a better way.

There is. The kids are angry because they can no longer play together. But there really is a better way of getting the children to know what you mean without your becoming the angry one in the room. Let's talk about what you can do the next time things get out of hand (and you know there will be a next time).

Here's what you gather so you might learn what the children hear you say. (Yes, so you can learn what they need to know.) Put identical things in two bags. By identical I mean perhaps two buttons, but they don't have to look exactly alike as long as they're identified as buttons; two wooden blocks that are the same color and shape, if possible (the shape and size don't have to be identical if you can't find them); two red blocks (although the colors can be different as long as there are two of each shape); and several other twosomes, one in each bag, that are similar in shape and meaning, such as two triangles that you may have to cut out of paper. Look around for what you need; about a dozen things will do.

Then get a board that will separate the two youngsters who will take part in this project. The board, or cardboard, should be large enough so that the two "players" won't be able to see each other. Choose two children to take part in this game, set them across from each other with the board between them, and you're ready to go.

Give each one a bag, and ask who wants to be the "adult" in charge of the room and who wants to be the "child." The adult is the only one who can talk; the child just has to listen and do as the adult tells her. No questions may be asked, and no further instructions may be given.

The "adult" picks one thing out of the bag and tells the "child" how and where to place hers on the table. The adult may say, "Put the blue block on the table facing me." Now the child may wonder how to do this, but she can't ask (in other words, can't talk back); she just does as she's told. The project goes on until all the things in the bag are gone.

Then the board is lifted, and the chances are the two sides will look very different. You see, the adult wasn't very clear about what he or she wanted the child to do. And because the child couldn't ask questions, she couldn't ask what the adult meant when giving directions.

The moral of the exercise is this: make sure your children understand what you want when you tell them what you mean. I've done this with many different kids and adults, and the exercise turns out the same. We just expect our children to understand us when sometimes it's not too clear what we mean. For example, if we say to put the toys away, we may have to explain exactly what we mean the first few times.

Let's Make an Apron

This is a great project, and your grandchildren will be proud of themselves after they've finished. You do need to know how to sew in order to complete this project.

Before you sit down with the kids, take a trip to a secondhand or thrift store. There you'll find a variety of valances from which to choose. Yep, curtain valances. One per child is what you'll need. (That is, unless you want to make pockets out of the same material; then you'll need two. If you only get one, get some other material, such as felt, that you can make the pockets out of.) Gather a large safety pin; some cording or strong or narrow ribbon that's eighteen inches longer than your grandchild's waist; and a needle and thread.

Attach the large pin to the end of the cord in such a way that it can withstand being pulled through the narrow rod hem of the valance. Start it for him or her, and then let the child push and pull the pin, with the attached cord, through to the other end of the material. If you see the child getting frustrated, you can help out, but don't take over if you don't need to.

Flatten the material, cut the pockets out of the second piece of material, and sew them onto the front, being careful not to sew up the rod side that the cord goes through. Once the cord or ribbon has gone through to the other side of the valance, flatten it, and tie thick knots in the cord beside both ends of the apron (to make sure the cord won't go back into the hem through which it was pulled), or simply tightly sew the end of each side so that the cord hanging from the valance will stay there. Now she has an apron!

Boys and girls can take part in this. Make sure you buy material that appeals to each child.

Huddling with Haiku

————◆————

You don't like poetry—or you just don't understand it. But stay with me a minute. You see, poetry can soothe the soul and give our grandchildren a look at life from a different point of view.

Haiku is an ancient form of Asian poetry. The poems are very short, written in a special fashion, and usually deal with how Mother Nature relates to human nature.

Lie on the floor, with your grandchildren tucked in beside you, and slowly read a haiku (pronounced "hi-koo") poem to them. Pause after each line. Ask for comments after you've read each poem. Ask them if the poem puts them in a special mood. Tell them there are no right or wrong answers to questions like this. This is so much fun.

There are books of haiku poems for children at your local library. You may also purchase inexpensive haiku books on the Internet and at local bookstores. Since you know your children's tastes, you may want to look through the book(s) ahead of time to know which poems might appeal to them.

The following poem, by Lee Gurga, easily puts one in a special kind of mood:

a bike in the grass

one wheel slowly turning—

summer afternoon

The above originally appeared in Fresh Scent:
Selected Haiku, Brooks Brothers
© 1998 by Lee Gurga
Permission granted by Lee Gurga for use by
Archway Publishing for Bonding with
Our Children in Fun and Easy Ways

59

The following poem appeared in Figtons Press in 1993 and was written by Garry Gay. Archway Publishing was granted permission to use this poem in Bonding with Our Children in Fun and Easy Ways.

Here's another special haiku, by Garry Gay:

after falling down

she asks for a bandaid

for her doll too

Now's a good time to explain that haiku poems don't rhyme, and tell the older children that they rarely use punctuation and usually follow a five-, seven- and five-syllable, three-line h-format. But this isn't all that important here.

When Eve, Alex, and I did this, the then seven-year-old Eve noted that the snow outside the window looked as if it was streaming in across the bright white of the dining room tablecloth. This is not haiku, but it did bring the outside in after having listened to the poems read beforehand. Seeing nature become part of our world planted a seed in her young mind.

Recently the girls wrote some poetry. Nine-year-old Eve created this work:

the moon shines bright over us

the sun gives us warmth all day

plants make oxygen to breathe

Alex came up with

the grass is always greener

the sun shines brighter

the water is clear and blue

Here are a few more haiku written by Lee Gurga:

first snow

little boy laughing

in his sleep

There's the comet …

the little boy watches

his father's breath

summer sunset—

the baby finds his shadow

on the kitchen wall

—First Prize, *Mainichi Daily News* Haiku Contest, 1991

Sunday afternoon

asking his father the name

of every flower

Wow, we grandparents sure work wonders—with something we know nothing about!

Crowd Control

You're reading a good novel in a comfortable chair. All is going along beautifully ... and then a blowup happens and chaos sets in. You're in charge, Nana, but now it's time to take charge.

Call a meeting. Everyone has to sit around the table, and everyone will have a chance to talk—but only after raising his or her hand. No tattling, no criticizing—just letting us know what's bothering you.

After all the negatives are out, recommendations will follow. With ownership of the problems come resolutions. Things will settle down. Now this may not last until Mom and Dad get home, but even a little peace and quiet go a long way.

Do Not Disturb

Our grandchildren rarely consider the fact that their parents often don't have much time together. Here's an idea that will take that into account: Do Not Disturb signs.

Cut some heavy paper into approximately six-by-four-inch pieces. If you decide to make the size a bit bigger, use the same proportions as above. Before you give each grandchild one, cut two holes in the edge of the top of the long end of the paper, and have each child thread a 20-inch piece of heavy string through one hole and out the other. Tie knots at the ends of the string (near the corners of the edges of the blank signs), and they are ready for the children to work on and then hang on a doorknob. Here the little ones will get a chance to feel what "wait and see" means as they sit patiently for the signs to be discovered.

If necessary, explain what "do not disturb" means, and spell the words if the younger children need help. With Magic Markers and colorful stickers, have the kids design their signs. A taste of creativity? A bit of peace for you while they work away? A surprise for their parents? This sounds like a home run to me!

Everyone Likes a Surprise

Using markers, glue, paper, ribbon, buttons, and, if necessary for the older kids, scissors, have each grandchild make up two fancy "I love you" cards, one for Mom and one for Dad. Then have them find spots to hide them: Mom's might be in the refrigerator and Dad's in his sock drawer. Most of all, tell the kids to be patient, and have them keep this a secret. After all, everyone likes a surprise!

On a different note, why not have the grandparents give each other a surprise? Grandma might put a love note in Grandpa's pocket when he's not looking, and Grandpa might just put Grandma's favorite candies in her purse. Surprise!

Let's Be Silly

———————◆————————

Silliness is so much fun! Sit around in a circle and say a sentence. This might be a good one for Mom to start with: "I rode my horse to the mall." Then the child to her left must say her silly sentence. Who knows what she'll say, especially after Mom's sentence was so funny. "I carried my dog to school." If all is going well, you might think of certain subjects that must be in everybody's sentence, such as the word "vacation." (If things get out of hand as far as topics or the choice of words goes, then the game is over.)

Even young children can play this game. Just be sure every sentence is silly. Jim, for instance, says, "My dog and I eat out of the same bowl, and we both like the same food."

Do you suppose they also sleep in the same bed? Laughs with the whole family are always fun.

Bag of Words

Be a bag lady: have a bag of words nearby. You never know when you'll need it, and we grandmothers always know when it's time to pull out something new. Grandpa can play this game too and come up with his own bag of words.

Beforehand, print words on small pieces of paper, fold them, and put them into a bag. When the game starts, take one out of the bag and read it to everyone.

Let's say the word is "fuzzy." Think of a funny sentence that includes the word: "Nick owns a fuzzy snake," or "Brianna loves fuzzy ice cream." Every child gets to make up a silly sentence using that particular word.

A variation of the game could have the children writing a goofy word and putting it in the bag just as you did.

And Then There's Music

It seems like the music our kids listen to is a mixture of atonal sounds and loud thumps. (See Mom and Dad nod their heads in agreement.) Let's introduce the kids to different kinds of music; they may not like any of it, but at least they'll have heard it.

One day put on country music. Try classical another time, and then jazz. Have everyone explain how and why he or she likes a certain kind of music.

A little research may help. Be sure to explain what your favorite kind of music is and where it comes from. If you can, show the children what kind of dance accompanies some kinds of music. (Don't be shy: even if you have two left feet, it's all in the family!) Explain that some music has no lyrics.

Have the children make up and sing funny words to songs they know, such as "The Farmer in the Dell." You and/or they might not want to listen to the sounds of different music, but at least you will all be introduced to something new.

After all, the adults love to tap their feet!

Fun Fonts

Every day, you're exposed to different styles of fonts. Compare a couple of kids' books, and you'll see what I mean. Wouldn't it be fun for our grandchildren to create their own font? It's easy.

First explain what a font is.

Demonstrate a bit of your printing skills. You can even make each letter in a word different from the others. Then give the kids markers and some paper and let them go at it. The older children may want to cut different letters out of old magazines or advertising in newspapers.

It doesn't matter what size, style, or color their fonts are. Shucks, some may print letters backward or upside down! Anything goes.

Try printing "I love you" in fun fonts.

Fun with Days

———◆———

Ever wish you could add a day or two to your week? How about deleting some obligations and adding enjoyment in their places? Mom'll let the kids do this at the same time. Just watch—and play along!

Give each child (and Mom) one large, blank, monthly calendar sheet and a pen. To give them an idea of what you're talking about, you go first. You might say that you love to shop and that you're going to mark off all the days you'd like to go to the mall. Then check two or three days a week you'd like to shop and maybe a few days when you'd like to sleep in late.

Everybody gets to check a day—or up to thirty-one—of their choice. Tim, for instance, may want to stay up late every evening of the month. And who wouldn't want a couple of birthdays a week? Okay, maybe not Mom, but she can always dream of eating out every day!

Be sure to put the checks on your calendars. If you don't have enough calendars, anyone else who wants to play can use a different color pen from yours so all can tell their different preferences. Do you think Mom and Dad have some things in common?

Is There a Dollhouse in the House?

Do your grandchildren have a dollhouse? If so, you're in luck. Get down on your hands and knees, Nana. This is one of those "good sport" projects. You may be surprised to find that the dollhouses of today are quite a bit different from the ones we had. They're more colorful, detailed, and often come with dolls and pools and many, many outfits.

Now's the time to pull out the "admiration quotes." "Hmm," you may say, "have you ever thought about getting some new carpeting for that beautiful living room?" Depending on her response you might say you'd be glad to check out a carpeting store to see if it has anything she may love. Don't forget to ask her color preference; often stores have small remnants that they practically give away. You might even find some grass green for the yard.

Don't forget to measure what size(s) you'll need. Now don't get carried away: it is her dollhouse. But if she has some ideas, you may want to get further involved.

She may ask you to play out a scene with one of her dolls. This is really fun, and she'll love you all the more for doing this.

Now comes the hard part: you must get up off the floor. But no whining aloud, Nana—although you may have to ask her to help you up.

Design a House for Me

S ay aloud, "Sometimes I wish I could design a new house for myself. Say—would you like to create one for me?"

Explain to the young ones how people first draw a floor plan before a house is built.

Pen and paper are all the kids need to fulfill your dreams. When I did this with our granddaughters, they created a luxury apartment for me in their own basement: they said they wanted me to live close to them! They drew every detail, including a bed next to mine for a dog they'd give me. I wonder if I should've told them I'd like a swimming pool.

In reality, my furnace is in the center of my real basement. But that didn't bother them; they just ignored it. They furnished the place, including flowers in the center of a table. The refrigerator door was open, but that didn't seem to bother anybody.

You might want to give this job to your little ones to see what they come up with. The older kids forgot to install a restroom, but once again no one worried about it.

How about a Group Hug?

W^e want and need hugs from our grandchildren. We'll know when it's time, so why don't we just say so? This includes any relatives who are in the house at this time. Heck, even "outsiders" could be included. After all, if you're here to be with our relatives, you're a temporary part of our family.

If the kids are in different rooms, let's ask them to join us in for one giant, all-together hug. The older ones might think this is a silly thing to do, but let's do it anyway. As a matter of fact, sharing a huge hug goes a long way.

Advertising Creativity

Have every child make his or her own signs. This is a good project for even young children; three-year-old Charlotte did this with a little help from her mom. Anything goes as far as merchandise or services are concerned. Kids may make a sign for anything they want to tell others about: "Pillows for Sale," "Buy a Green Toy," or "Cookies," for example. Perhaps Mom might get the hint here, and who knows what may come from this sign? Charlotte's mom came up with a batch of chocolate chips, and her daughter loved them. The choices are endless. Again, Magic Markers and paper are all you need. Hang the signs all around the house.

Charlotte paid attention to what the signs said. She figured some of the things the kids put up for sale they might have outgrown and were tired of having around. Maybe it was time to get some new toys.

One thing the kids don't really know is that they're advertising their creativity. Saying things in written words also shows that they are growing up.

Tear Up the Rug

Let the good times roll—dance! And not only you: have everybody move their feet.

Pick out a spot for the stage, put the music on high, and then everyone—one at a time—gets a chance to perform.

Grandmother goes first. Twist, tap-dance, belly dance, ballet—you name it. And then, after everyone has had a chance to show off, all of you dance your own dance—at the same time.

Go for it, Grandma. You can tear up the rug like nobody's business!

Dream Aloud with Me

All kids love make-believe. Create a dream for tonight. You go first. Your dream might include a new car, a trip to the mountains, or shopping for a colorful dress. Castles and puppets and chocolate galore might be his, and spaceships and a pet dog might be hers. You may dream about something that will really happen or something truly ridiculous. And who says you can't have more than one dream?

Ask the children what they think their family members might dream tonight. Mom starts. She might say that Alex will dream that she will learn to ski on their upcoming trip. After all the dream guesses are shared, Mom might tell which ones are closest to her dreams and maybe share some dreams she might have that nobody came close to. I think at least one child will dream about having a pet.

Dreaming aloud sure is fun.

Who's Who

———— ◆ ————

Who's who in your grandchildren's world is far different from who was who in yours when you were young. Are Dale Evans and Lassie still around? We may know less about who's who today than we think we do.

Sit down with your grandchildren and find out who their favorite cartoon characters are, who their favorite singers are, and so on. Why not ask the child to sing one of his or her favorite singer's songs, or act like the cartoon character he or she likes? The kids will be impressed that you care enough to ask. But be ready to act like Dale Evans, just as Grandmother Ruthie had to! Her grandchildren Mike and Amy thought she was a real star.

Personalized Wearable Art

Remember tie-dying T-shirts? Everyone here can create a colorful T-shirt without making a mess. Here's what we need:

- A washed, plain T-shirt for everyone who's taking part in this fun project. The shirts can be found in secondhand stores or even at display tables in drugstores.
- Fabric dye. This is the "paint" you'll use. Small plastic containers are sold at fabric and craft supply stores. They are inexpensive and often on sale. You don't need many colors—even one will do. These dyes are safe for children to use.
- Clothes hangers for drying the finished products.
- Plenty of plastic for aprons and a tablecloth.

The kids will use the dyes like they do markers. They can draw shapes, animals, flowers, flags, hearts, their names—anything they want. The ink is permanent, so remind the kids that once the dye is on a shirt, it cannot be erased. Hang the shirts until the ink dries completely. Then wash the clothing before the kids wear it. Soap and hot water won't remove the designs.

Wouldn't it be terrific if all the adults made one for him- or herself? Uh-oh, here we go again. We should all be good sports. And don't forget: making one means wearing it.

Writing Backward

Whether our little grandchildren can print or not, they can still play this game. Stick figures drawn in action poses will also do the trick.

Have everyone print his or her name in reverse order on a piece of paper. Not only from the right to the left, but making each letter backward. When, for instance, an "e" is printed backward, it will look like "ɘ." Once they get it, the older children will be able to do this on their own. The younger ones may need your help.

When each is finished, have him or her hold up his or her paper with the printed side turned toward a mirror. Every child will be delighted to see what's printed or drawn.

You've done it again—some magic for all to see and do.

Boxes, Boxes, Boxes

When I was a kid my parents couldn't afford many toys for us, but they were clever enough to bring home large boxes. What fun we had pretending those boxes were all kinds of things: stores, cribs, schoolhouses, and more.

Tired of seeing your kids only playing with commercially made toys—or toys that don't require much imagination? Get some large boxes. You can go to a department, furniture, or appliance store—really, almost any retail store. Employees will often break them down for you so they'll fit in your car. Take them to your grandchildren's house, along with some markers, and let their imaginations go to work. You'll all have a day or two's worth of big-time fun.

After consideration, Eve and Alex decided they wanted a pet shop. Using a box cutter, Grandpa cut out a big window and added a shelf. The girls worked together when it came to decorating the walls, pricing the animals, making a sign, and displaying the dogs. Eve staffed the store. She brought out all the girls' stuffed animals. When the store opened, Eve hummed to the dogs, brushed their fur out, and dusted the shop.

This little show took a long time to set up. Once they set a goal, they worked well together.

Along came Alex carrying one of her mom's purses. She stopped to look at Eve's dogs and then sang the song "How Much Is That Doggie in the Window?" Eve put the largest dog on the shelf, and Alex fell in love with it. She paid for it with homemade money, and all of us were happy! We all had a fine time.

Get some boxes and see what can be done with them. I'll bet you too can make an afternoon, or more, out of them.

Cleaning Up by Color

Picking up toys is nobody's favorite job, and kids seem to dislike it even more than Mom does. For a change, try having them do it by color. Not only will the job get done, but the children will have fun doing it. But either grandparents or Papa has to help. For this to work it has to be a secret from Mom until everything is cleaned up. You'll see.

Have Mom go into another room so she won't see what's going on, and then have your grandchildren put away every red toy in the cluttered room in which they were playing. When Mom is called back to the playroom, she has to guess what's happened. Now she won't guess this time, so she has to go out and the kids choose a different color. Maybe it'll be blue this time.

This is repeated until Mom guesses what's going on. And if she's smart, she won't acknowledge that she's figured it out until the entire room is cleaned up! And the grandparents and Papa are just as happy as the children's mother.

Come Fall ...

C ome fall there are so many beautiful leaves of all different colors lying on the ground and hanging low on trees. It seems such a waste not to enjoy them in the house.

There are several ways to dry them out, all the while maintaining their beautiful colors. All it takes is wax paper; a cookie sheet or flat wooden board; paper towels or some other soft, thin towel; and an iron.

Take the grandchildren outside to collect pretty leaves. Have them choose those with no tears or holes in them, with complete edges all around, with stems, and are brightly colored. Have the children either hold them flat or give them to you to do so.

After you have the number of leaves you want, head for the house. There you will dry them as much as you can, using soft rags or towels to do the job. Then place the dry leaves on wax paper on a flat surface. Cookie sheets do the trick; leaves also stay out of the way if you place them on your kitchen countertop.

Place another sheet of wax paper on top of the leaves. Make the paper as flat as you can. The last step is again placing a towel or rag on top of this side too.

Then turn your iron on low, and press down firmly for two to five minutes. After that, turn the leaves and attached wax paper over onto the wax paper that you had placed on the other side of the leaves. Put the towel on the leaves as before, and press the iron on it. It probably won't take as many minutes this time because chances are the leaves have dried by this time.

After the leaves have cooled off, remove the towels or rags, and trim around the leaves' edges, being careful to not create holes where air can get in and spoil your project. If the leaves are firm enough, you can gently peel the wax paper off completely, but you have to work carefully.

There are other ways to wax leaves, but they include items you need to purchase. Even waxing leaves without using purchased items, the colors stay beautiful for a very long time. The kids can have fun decorating the house with the leaves—and so can we.

Being a Grandmother

---◆---

It was a pleasant day. I walked to the corner where the girls' school bus dropped them off. Since I got there a few minutes early, I sat on the curb. Soon I heard gushing water under the sewer grating beneath my feet. Then, looking up, I saw a bird walking sideways on a rooftop. Soon a nearby weed caught my eye: on one leaf was a round raindrop from an earlier shower. It hadn't yet slipped away in the sun. I couldn't wait to show my granddaughters.

The bus came and the girls jumped off. They rushed over to give me big hugs and then walked ahead toward the house, chattering away.

Sometimes grandmothers are with their grandchildren. Sometimes grandmothers are alone. Sometimes grandmothers are gathering up beauty to be shared later. Sometimes grandmothers are just grandmothers, and that's beautiful in itself.

Enjoy.

Confidence-Building Tips for Being Good Role Models

Let your grandchildren see you donate to a charity, even if your donation is small. It's the action that counts.

Take some brownies to a fire station; introduce yourself to a neighbor who lives down the street; ask to talk to the manager of a bakery to give her a personal compliment. If you're able, take some flowers when you go on your visits. Expand and enjoy your world.

Have a photo of your mom and dad in your house for your grandchildren to see.

Take a tour of your city or a nearby one, an art museum, a courthouse. Being curious will show your grandchildren that this is a fine trait to have.

Talk to your plants while watering them. You'll feel positive vibrations when you do.

If you're 55 or older, ask for senior discounts. You'd be surprised at how many establishments give them. Some don't even advertise them; you just have to ask. Even if you look young, don't hesitate. You can whisper your request.

Word-of-mouth is a good way to find out about interesting events in your community. Ask questions.

Give yourself a birthday party. Send invitations to friends and family. Ask them to come celebrate life with you. No gifts, please.

Don't make anybody feel guilty. Save your energy for better things.

Don't be humiliated to poke around for good deals. You'd be surprised at what you can find in the 80 percent off bin at a hardware store, or on the sale racks at a department store. End-of-season sales are often great places to find gifts and items for the kids and your projects with them.

Become a Scout leader. You may be able to participate at your local school even if your grandchildren aren't students there. Don't worry; the Scouts will train you.

Curiosity abounds. You have questions to ask your grandchildren, and they have questions to ask you. Share with them, but you know where to draw the line.

A letter to the editor of your local newspaper may result in change.

Contact the politicians who represent you to find out what's going on about something you're interested in.

Volunteer. You might end up on a committee—and that's time well spent.

Don't have a car, or don't want to drive somewhere? Lots of communities and organizations offer low-cost or free rides for senior citizens.

Surprise your grandchildren's parents: volunteer to babysit. Don't wait for their anniversary or one of their birthdays.

Barter. If you bake a mean chocolate cake and a friend or a neighbor can fix a dripping faucet, you're in business. Or ask to borrow something—and return it with some cookies attached. The possibilities are endless.

Keep a book in plain sight in your car. This is good for two reasons: it'll give you something to read while you're waiting for an appointment, and your grandchildren will see how important reading is to you.

Join an animal rescue society or volunteer for one. Your grandchildren will think you're really cool for doing this.

Visit an art museum. Even if you don't count art as one of your favorites, make an effort to go. An art exhibit at a gallery or an art street fair is good too. (You aren't expected to buy anything. You may walk away bewildered, but that's okay. It'll be great when the kids realize you're actively exploring culture.)

Feeling sorry for yourself? That's all right, but try this: give yourself 15 minutes to really feel sorry for yourself. When the time is up, it's up. Carry on with feeling better. Don't let things keep you down.

Save up to buy a charity T-shirt or a library book bag. Or take a free bookmark from the library or a bookstore.

Don't throw anything out until you consider its value for any future project.

Put your grandchildren's photos, handwritten notes, drawings, and/or cards on your refrigerator. They are the best decorations you can have. And don't forget to ask for updates.

A grandchild wants to tell you a secret. Honor your promise to not tell anyone. However, if it's a really serious matter, tell the child he or she must tell his or her parents and that you'll be by the child's side throughout.

Even if you see your grandchildren often, once in a while send them an e-mail message, a letter, or a postcard. Personal mail is always fun to get. You can just say hi.

Keep your mind sharp. Play games, do crossword or word-search puzzles, play cards.

Take a minute to think about your parents and grandparents. Did/ do they dance and laugh often? Did/do they do anything that you might want to do with your grandchildren?

Use the gifts your children and grandchildren give you even if they are unusual. You do want to learn how to do magic tricks and to cook Chinese food, don't you? After you learn, giving a demonstration, with all the bells and whistles, would make that child feel special.

Send a letter to the publisher of a book that is really good for the kids. Don't know who to send it to? Look on the Internet or ask the local reference librarian. Let your grandchildren know you're doing this. As a matter of fact, include a thank-you, even if it's a drawing from them.

Try doing a small repair job without first calling a handyman. You may not succeed, but your efforts will be admired by your grandchildren. If they're old enough (even if they're not), let them help out. If you can't fix it, let the kids see you making arrangements with someone who can. Asking for help when you really need it is a good trait.

Become an expert at something. Does this mean you should become a professional pianist? No way. Learn how to tie string into great shapes, complete a needlepoint project, or learn the words to a popular song.

Can't afford the price of a movie ticket? Check out your local library. It may schedule free movies for members of the community or lend out DVDs or videos like they do books. Libraries are full of things to do: some offer crocheting and knitting classes; chess clubs;

or book reading groups. Most of these meetings don't last more than 90 minutes.

Even if you are financially strapped, you don't have to say a word: be proud. Walk the walk, talk the talk. If anyone thinks you're less than he or she is, that's the other person's problem. It's his or her loss.

Erase the phrases "should have" and "if only" from your vocabulary. They get in the way of solving problems.

Attend your city or borough meetings. Speak out about issues that are important to you.

Enjoy your life. Enjoy the time you have with your children and grandchildren no matter how long or short it is.

Printed in the United States
By Bookmasters